This Book is dedicated to daughter. Thank you for giving me the courage to write this. Sam, you have been my rock through this whole journey and my true best friend, my pain is your pain, my happiness is your happiness, and I wouldn't want to do this life with anyone else. My daughter, I hope one day when or if read this, you'll come to realise how truly special you are to us and that maybe my experiences will help you in your walk-through womanhood and perhaps, hopefully one day, motherhood.

Warning – This book contains graphic descriptions of medical procedures, miscarriages, and suicidal thoughts which some may find destressing

Introduction

It's the start of a new year, January 2022 and I'm questioning whether I should even be writing this book. It's deeply personal and painful and it will require all the bravery I can muster to express honestly and truthfully all that my family have experienced. The more people I speak to, women on the most part, and interestingly those who work beside me in the various healthcare professions, have been shocked by my journey and have had no idea these things could happen, how they've happened and what is truly involved. It was one comment by a friendly female colleague who said to me.

"I wish I had known all this, and that women were educated more on these subjects because I would have no idea where to start, where to go or how to make things happen if it were me."

So here I am baring my heart and soul so that maybe my experiences can help and guide those who need it but also, more importantly, if I can comfort just one person then it'll all be worth it.

Chapter One – Young Love

I met my husband seventeen long years ago and we've been married for fourteen of them. I can honestly say he's my absolute best friend, although, he does drive me nuts on a few occasions! I knew pretty quickly that he was the one who I wanted to share everything with and, luckily for me, he felt the same way. To say we've been on a journey to have a family is a understatement. Like most couples we had dreams of starting a family fairly quickly after getting married. We planned on three, maybe four children depending on our circumstances and loving anything that needs organising, I dreamt of charts on the wall of afternoon clubs, holidays and sporting events all mapped neatly out for each child. I was going to be the new Kris Jenner – well, perhaps not that extreme!

I remember as clear as day, the first time we stopped using protection. I was as nervous as a person about to do a bungy jump off a bridge. I remember saying to my husband "You know, we could get pregnant, right now!?" Was this right? Could we handle it? Was this a good decision?

Believe me, for other couples we know, this is how it happens. You have a roll in the hay once, maybe a few times that month and presto the next month you're expecting. I swear one of our friends has to pass her husband on the stairs and she gets pregnant!

But, alas, not for us, we managed three, going on four years of trying. Then in 2012 we decided to go to see our GP.

In the meantime, the usual 'helpful' loving comments rolled in…

"Are you sure you're doing IT right?"

"It's ok we tried for a long time too, it took like three months before we got pregnant…"

"Perhaps you should get blindingly drunk and have a one-night stand!"

People have no clue the hurt those statements can do. I quickly learnt to deal with people's insensitivities and figured the only way to move on from them (or rather not listen to them) was to realise they had no experience of true infertility issues.

I think some people have children too quickly or don't fully understand how much a child turns your life upside down and inside out. I've seen it plenty of times before. They pop them out, one after the other, and then wonder why they have no money, can't work like they used to and their old social life doesn't exist. They whine and moan about their children, with almost a tinge of regret. To someone who is going through infertility, this is like a dagger to the heart and, makes you mad, very very mad. How can people disregard what an unbelievable precious gift they've been given? BREATHE. They are allowed to express their feelings as much as you are but, again, it's the insensitive factor you have to remind yourself of. They don't know or understand what you're going through. There is something to be said about waiting a little longer than most to have a child. It brings the word 'appreciation' to a whole new level.

Chapter Two – Tests, Tests and What do men do?

In the summer of 2012, me and my husband booked an appointment to see our GP.

"How can I help you today?" he asked.

"Well, we've been trying for a baby and it's just not happening for us."

"How long have you been trying?" he asked.

"Three, coming up four years."

LONG PAUSE.

"Gosh, that is a long time to be trying, lets get you booked in for some tests."

When I look back on it, he was right. Three to four years is a long time to keep trying. Most couples approach their healthcare professional after a few months, maybe a year. I'm not really sure why we waited that long. To be honest, we were still fairly young at this point and we were happily living our lives. Trying for a baby, it seemed like, a normal part of marriage but as the years ticked by, we slowly reached our desperation point. Others reach it much sooner than we did and rightly so. The quicker you get tested, the sooner you could find a reason to your problems.

So, we were booked into our local hospital. I had no clue what was going to happen or what I was being tested for and what methods they would use – having not researched or read up on anything (As I meticulously do now in my wiser years, for EVERYTHING!) I trusted the experts and what they thought was needed to be done, so we just went along for the ride.

Can I just stop for a moment and make a statement. At this point – MEN – you are the luckiest species on earth when it comes to making babies or having fertility tests. All a man needs to do is enjoy himself for a few minutes to produce a sample of his swimmers, and Bob's your uncle, that's their part done! I mean, how unbelievably unfair is this? There's actual PLEASURE involved on their part in this. Under no circumstances is pleasure included in any women's testing. Moan over.

After my husband had dropped his sample into the hospital at a specific time, it was my turn. I had the first of my three scheduled examinations. Number one was a follicle tracking (follicle, meaning production of eggs) and wellness scan.

I have what is called a retroverted womb, meaning it tips slightly backwards which can make things a little harder to see on a regular ultrasound. So, every scan I now must have (I know this now after having had endless amounts of them years later!) are done vaginally. This involves having a large cold probe stuck up in between your legs and it's moved around to have a good look at your insides. The first time for me was painful, not because of the scanning itself or the equipment, but because of the person who was doing the actual examining. As already mentioned, I've had countless examinations done in my lifetime and I've never found them to be painful in any way, just a slight discomfort at times. It just so happens on that particular day, at that particular hospital, this particular nurse decided to take her frustrations with life out on me. She barely spoke a word to me except "Lie down, spread your legs." There was no explanation as to what was going on and why she was doing what she was doing. At one point I said 'Ouch'. She ignored me and continued to route around with the probe any way she wished. She couldn't even crack a smile or, dare I say, apologise for causing me pain.

"You have two eggs." She said.

Was that a good thing? Was it a bad thing? I was lying there too scared to ask.

"Wipe yourself down and wait in reception."

What the heck just happened?

Honestly, after that experience I was lucky to carry on our fertility journey. Were all my appointments going to be like this? Thankfully, I can say absolutely not. Most nurses I have come into contact with have been wonderful, caring and sensitive. This one was not.

Can I just address those uncaring individuals right now… I understand that seeing endless vaginas day in day out can get a little tiresome but please understand each woman you see is an individual. We are not wombs on a conveyor belt (That's how I felt!) It was my first EVER examination. I was scared, nervous and at this point uneducated about the whole process. Just a little compassion and kindness can go a very long way.

Luckily, I never saw this nurse again. As I left the room a lovely lady at reception gave me an information leaflet (which would have been helpful beforehand!) including an appointment to come back in a weeks' time to see if I was ovulating.

This usually happens on day ten to sixteen of your cycle (depending on if your cycles are regular) So make yourself flexible for this as it matters a great deal.

Back I go to the hospital a week later for more prodding and poking only to be told all looks good apparently.

In the past I have had male professionals do examinations on me also. I appreciate for some women this would make them feel very uncomfortable and that is completely understandable. However, I have found them to be incredibly compassionate. They have been much more sensitive and gentler than their female colleagues. Sometimes I think women have the misconception that all females go through these things, therefore just get on with it. This stoic approach is archaic and can be quite frankly dangerous. It must not be allowed to happen.

We were asked to wait in reception where we would be called to the specialist's office to go through the results. My husband and I were next. We sat in the clean white office of the lead female consultant for a short time before she came and gave us the outcome.

"Sir, your test has come back, and I'm pleased to say they're very good. You're super fertile!"

Well, I wish I had a camera at that moment to take a picture of my husband's face. He was like the Cheshire cat, grinning from ear to ear. It was as if his manliness (if there is such a thing!) had been proven that day. His seed was good. So good in fact, that he proceeded to message all his male friends later that day bragging about his so-called super sperm! (Insert rolling eye face here!)

"Madam, your results were also good. We can see from your scans that you have a number of follicles in your ovary and two eggs were present and you are indeed ovulating as normal."

Fantastic we thought, but then we were hit with that feeling most couples experience when they get great results (which is not always a good thing when you're having fertility issues – strange I know.) If there's something wrong, you can fix it. So, were do WE go from here when everything seems right?

"However, since you've been trying so long to get pregnant and it's not happened yet, we will suggest putting you on Clomid ... an ovulation stimulating drug."

I was then given a handful more leaflets about what was involved and was discharged with a prescription for three months' worth of the drug. I would have to take it on specific days of my cycle to make my ovaries produce more eggs. No problem I thought... I was wrong.

Chapter Three – The Monster in me, more tests for me, Why me!?

'Mittelschmerz' is a funny word. It's what professionals refer to as ovulation pain. The sensation of sharp pain on one or both sides of your womb where you can almost feel a grape like something where your ovary sits as an egg is being released. Thankfully it passes after a day or so and is normal for most women during their ovulation phase.

Month one, ovulation stage and I popped the pills. Oh, my days, Clomid for me was horrific. First came the pain and then something worst happened. I turned into the incredible hulk. I got all bloated, green from nausea and angry – so, so angry at everyone and everything. My poor husband, he described me as evil incarnate when I took these tablets. Can I just point out that, although side affects are common when taking clomid, mine were pretty extreme. Everyone reacts differently to these things – unfortunately mine involved me turning into a rageful Frankenstein's monster. I was stomping around in a cloud of rage (Limp Bizkit music never sounded so good) and my husband was tiptoeing around me on eggshells and we had to approach the subject of love making. Oh, yes, we were trying for a baby and that involved us being intimate. You know, the romantic, loving, making another human being kind of intimacy. But I didn't want to be touched let alone have sex, and I know for sure my husband didn't want to go near me either for fear of me ripping his head clean off. So, we did what any other couple desperate to get pregnant does – you have that mechanical liaison where neither of you wants to be there, but you know you have to for scientific purposes. Is this how we really wanted to make a baby?

"Of course dear, you were conceived on a romantic night celebrating our wedding anniversary…" BIG FAT LIE. Thank goodness we only had three months of the stuff because if we had gone on any longer it would have ended up with me joining the Avengers or, joking aside, in divorce. Luckily my husband knew it was the drugs talking, it made me into someone I wasn't when we could have done with the real me being in the room. He saw past the Clomid induced rages, but I know he was considering reaching for the lawyer's number. As you can probably guess, we didn't get pregnant and not for, I think, medal worthy trying on our part. (A special bravery award for my husband too!) In fact, I later found out, clomid has a pretty poor rate of success. At tops 38% fall pregnant on Clomid. I wish I had been in that percentage.

Back to the consultant we went, not knowing what our choices were or if there were any moving forward. The last examination would be the most unpleasant (but luckily is only done once) and that was a Hysterosalpingogram (HSG). You lay awake under an x ray machine, while a doctor slides a catheter up your fallopian tubes, inserts some dye and watches on the x-ray screen as the dye slides its way back out. The dye will show if there's any blockages or abnormalities which can stop an egg reaching your womb.

"Hang on a minute. Why didn't I have this done first? Surely, I should have had this BEFORE going on Clomid!? What's the point in trying with ovulation drugs if the egg can't even get through!?"

If you're starting your fertility journey, please bring this to your specialists' attention. IT MAKES NO SENSE and wastes months, potentially years of trying on your part for nothing if your tubes are not right!

I'm sure my description doesn't sound too pleasant, but it was fine. Again, a male doctor did the procedure, and he was fantastic. Gentle, slow, kind and explained at every stage what he was doing. He was even jolly which helped my anxiety immensely. My husband looked on from the corner of the room horrified. I'm sure it looked a lot worse than it felt. Most doctors tell you to take the day off to rest as afterwards because it's like having a mini period, except your sanitary towel is a little blue rather than red and your cramps are tense but pass after a short time. I stupidly went straight to work afterwards, where I stand up all day. Big mistake. If you have to have this procedure, relax, take the whole day off. Buy lots of chocolate and sit on the sofa with a hot water bottle binge watching reality tv.

Here we go again. My results were all clear. No problems. The consultant said they could do one of two things. One of them they couldn't do on the NHS because success rates were not high enough for them to fund. This is called IUI, or officially Intrauterine insemination. This is where the partners sperm is injected through a catheter into the uterus, or as close as they can to the ovary, at the time you're ovulating (much like the procedure

I had to check if my fallopian tubes were blocked). I quite liked this idea but unfortunately it wasn't an option at that time and with a 13% success rate you can understand them taking this off the table. Now it was down to our last and final route. IVF.

For those couples out there, that go through IVF (Invitro fertilisation) I whole heartedly applaud you. You are absolute warriors. In my circle of friends/colleagues/family we know of a few success stories but also some heart-breaking unsuccessful ones.

The decision to do IVF is not one that should be taken lightly. We were one of the lucky ones that were offered three rounds for free, but it was a lot to consider. Did we really want to do this? By this point we were both exhausted from all the investigations and the month after month of trying. We needed a break to protect ourselves and our relationship.

IVF is all consuming. You need to take (and/or inject) lots of medications, be monitored with scans throughout your cycle. That's not including the procedure to remove your eggs (when you've had them stimulated beforehand with drugs like Clomid) then you have them implanted once fertilised meticulosity under a microscope. I'm paraphrasing, there is so much involved. It will take over your life once you're in that cycle. I know one person who it worked for on the first try and I'm delighted for them, but I also know of others who after many attempts it didn't, and this is devastating. You put all your energy, time, efforts and for some, all your money and it can still not work out. IVF seems to put all the things in the right place at the right time to make it happen but if only it were that simple. At the moment the success rate is around 32% but of course this can be higher or lower depending on age, lifestyle, and health factors. It is a huge decision to undertake and a lot to ask of your body. I wish it worked every time for anyone going down this path, but we were acutely aware that many times it didn't.

At this point, most couples have already tried various ways to get pregnant and have been trying for a considerable amount of time before reaching an IVF decision. May I strongly advise if you're one of these people, take a step back to access how your relationship is at this time. You need to be in this together 110% because IVF is even more of an emotional rollercoaster than anything else. There's nothing wrong with taking a breath, having a break or even an actual holiday. Don't react out of desperate emotions. Protect your relationship first because, after all, it's the foundation and the reason you want to bring a child into this world. You can come back to see how you feel in a month or two. It CAN wait. You'll be better and stronger for it should you wish to proceed. But of course, if you go for it straight away then I wish you all the love in the world.

We had been at this for FIVE years now and a little sunshine and relaxation is exactly what we needed before we made our next decision. We had to choose the right path for us.

Chapter Four – Adoption… It runs in the Family

Years ago, we went to church most Sundays and at that time we were part of a wonderful congregation that shared life together. A family in the church, who had adopted recently, arranged for a local authority to do a presentation on adoption. After all the years of trying and specialists finding nothing wrong with either of us, was this the answer to us growing our family? We listened intently and at the end grabbed an information pack. My husband was very positive from the onset but I on the other hand needed some time. In my head, going for adoption was giving up on having a natural child. That might seem like a crazy thing to say and, how hurtful on the potential adopted child. It's not. For a woman, it's a huge thing to accept, or not so much accept, but rather to make peace with. You have to find a way to close that chapter and focus on the next one. Do it when you're ready. Don't force it and feel you have to – everyone comes to their own conclusion in their own way and if you don't want to or can't, then that's ok too. However, if this is something you're struggling with then I strongly advise you to seek out a medical professional or counsellor who can help you work through these feelings. It really will help to make sense of your emotions and how best to channel them.

After a little time and having felt after all these years, that a 'biological' child for us didn't seem to be on the cards for us, I was able to look at adoption as an exciting next step and made the necessary phone calls to get the ball rolling.

I would like to stop a moment and make a statement that needs to be said. Please don't approach adoption with a fairy tale dream like expectation. It's not like deciding to get a dog from the RSPCA, where you know there's going to be teething problems, but that dog will eventually complete your family and it's quick and easy.

"Just pick out the one you like the most, take it home and job done.!"

It's NOTHING like this! And rightly so. This is a child you're talking about. A precious child who, devastatingly, is in the system for a reason. A reason you need to be prepared for, along with everything else you may not have thought about. Adoption can be hugely successful and is an absolutely wonderful event – I have my own family members that are proof of this! But as I share with you the true preparation work that goes into adoption, always bare this in mind….. An adopted child does not change to fit into your lifestyle, you change for them.

The process took us over a year to complete and opened our eyes to many things we hadn't considered but, oh boy were we glad we did it. It's 100% right that it takes this long and I'm sure my re-telling will make it clear why. Plus the fact, you do wonder to yourself – if all prospective parents had this kind of training before they became a family maybe our society would be that much better. It's invaluable.

In November 2014 we started stage one, of three, of the adoption process. The first step includes the initial assessment as a couple, a stage one training event, general checks and references. This in reality should take two months tops, but obviously can take a little longer. We were assigned a lovely social worker who came to our house and she basically carried out an interview on us.

That morning I went into total panic mode for not having any biscuits in the house… Who has a guest and doesn't have biscuits to offer them with their cup of tea!? I sent my husband out to rush to the nearest shop to fetch some! Thank God for custard creams!

She asked us what we did for a living, what our hobbies were, what we did in our spare time etc etc. It was quite nice really, having a chat about ourselves and our stories. We felt very encouraged for the future. We were then told we needed full police and medical checks to be done next and three personal references (two of which could not be related to us). She would confidentially interview each of the references without us being present in order to get a complete view of us as individuals and as a couple.

We booked in with our GP to have full health checks done. No problems. Then we submitted our reference suggestions. One set of parents, our then current pastor and his wife and our closest friends at the time. We obviously had to pre-warn them that a social worker would be in contact to arrange interviews with them to talk about us. So, naturally, we bribed them with cake to say the nicest things – JOKE!!! Still to this day we have absolutely no idea what was asked/said in these meetings. We didn't receive and feedback afterwards but were soon after invited to attend the next stage, an information evening, so we assumed nice things were indeed said. Thanks guys!

The information evening/training was very laid back. More a sit and listen and takes notes kind of event. They covered points on why you were thinking of adopting/neglect/case studies/ children in care/ the future, the subject matters you would expect to learn more on at this point. Not long after, we were delighted to be told by our social worker that we had been successful in moving forward to stage two. What a relief!

We were told at this point we could take a break if we wanted to. In fact, in between each stage you can take a breather for up to six months. We were a little puzzled by this – why take a break now? This is all going great, and we couldn't wait to adopt. But we hadn't yet reached the next chapter and, my oh my, we understood what she meant by then. Stage two is seriously intense. Be prepared to have your life turned upside down and inside out. Remember the lovely interview we had in stage one? Yea, that was the slow journey up the tracks before the rollercoaster plunges you over the edge taking you on a mad ride of emotion for the next six months.

She came and stayed… for hours. Including interviewing us separately. No stone was left unturned and rightly so. If these people were going to be handing us a child at the end of this process (fingers and toes crossed) then they really, and I mean really needed to know who we were, past, present and future.

From the copy of the report I still have in my files we covered almost sixteen different subjects! Family background, education, work, health issues, relationship networks, community, housing, finances, experiences with children, your identity, past experiences, ability to sustain your relationship, emotional openness, support, tolerance but to name a few. I distinctly remember her asking 'How did this/that influence you?' repeatedly. Eek! You may be reading this and thinking, crikey that's a lot to take and quite frankly downright frightening. Well, in a manner of speaking, yes it was. I had to stop on several occasions to have a breather, or rather cry and reach for the box of tissues. But remember the end goal here. This is not only about you – it's about the child that your potentially ging to adopt. Can you truly provide them with that they need? You cannot have any secrets or skeletons in your closet because this process intents to find them out. There were things I absolutely didn't want to share but I felt it necessary because it showed my true self, my vulnerabilities and honesty.

Let me tell you, it means the world to have a wonderful social worker who you connect with, who you really like and trust whole heartedly because it makes this part so much easier. To be honest it was like having an extra-long session on the couch with 'a therapist' or a marriage counsellor. It was exhausting, and I know some people who have gone through this and enjoyed the whole process. But for us, in the end, we found it all quite cathartic. Looking back, it was absolutely essential. Adoption (even parenting in general) can bring up so many more challenges than you expect, and you've got to have you "stuff" together.

I believe, in part, this could be why so many couples break up. If this sort of stuff doesn't get properly addressed and you add a chid to the mix where stresses and strains come to the forefront, it's easy to see how it becomes too much for the relationship and you part ways. You cannot do this when you adopt. The child would have already experienced separation, even/and neglect and needs to be placed in a forever home – emphasises on FOREVER.

When this is complete, along with other random friendly visits your social worker decides to make, the report is submitted to an adoption panel. In the meantime, we attend a two-day training course. We drove to a village hall around an hour away and were greeted by several social workers (ours did not attend – this is not vital) and met several other potential adopters. There was a great mix of young and older couples, some already had children, some who did not, same sex couples and a single parent. It was a wonderful group to be a part of. The training was almost like a team building day you go on with your work colleagues, with the slide shows and PowerPoints mixed in. But the topics covered here were real tough ones. This was reality biting. The first sessions were on things such as diversity/identity and 'what if' scenarios. We got to hear adoption stories that had both good and bad outcomes.

Then there was the abuse video. It was a dad beating his son. It was brief but enough to make me leave the room for a second, as I found it really upsetting to watch. The police interviewed the dad afterwards and his response really opened my eyes. I remember him saying,

"My own father beat me so what wrong was I doing?"

It clearly showed that a situation like this in society is all too common in our society and is a vicious cycle which needs to be broken. I truly was educated in a way I wasn't expecting to be.

Seeing these true scenarios is incredibly important. An adoption also affects a large group of people. It's not just you, your spouse (if you have one) and this child live happily ever after. There is a past, a whole other family unit to think of and sometimes adoption is very painful for the birth parent(s). Every story is different and needs to be listened to and understood no matter how hard it is, regardless of your own personal opinions or beliefs.

Moving on, we learnt more on the subject of neglect, separation and attachment. All equally important because these are topics that as prospective parents you don't usually give a huge amount of thought on. This child you're wanting to make part of your lives has already lived – and in a lot of cases not a nice existence. You need to understand and apply how that is going to affect them and you as a family. Again, as I stated beforehand, a child does not fit into your lifestyle, you change for them. I will stand by this statement always. You need to see the world through their eyes.

Although extremely tough there were also aspects of great fun during our training. For example, we had to pitch a tent as a couple from scratch whilst being watched and evaluated by these ladies with their clipboards. It's pretty hilarious, trying not to shout at your beloved for putting the wrong pole in the wrong place by just using your glaring eyes! Every time you saw someone watching you would lovingly smile at your partner. Even though you know they can see right through all that, you do it anyways!

At the end of all the training we finished with a session on adopted children. We had a group of people, young and old who talked openly to us about their journey to adoption, how they felt about their birth parents (and if they still had contact with them) to how life was with their adoptive family. We even had an adult man talk about his past, his present and now that's he's an adult how adoption has affected his life. It was fascinating and we were able to ask questions (within reason) on things we wanted to know more on. It was an invaluable interaction and again brought aspects to the forefronts of our minds we had not contemplated. We left those training sessions, transformed. We were not the same people going into that hall as we were coming out and I truly believe it was for the better. I wish all adults, prospective parents or not should do this regardless because our understanding, empathy and love grew tenfold. Yes, this process is tough, but it's meant to weed out the weak from the strong. You need to be strong when you adopt. The challenges are different when you have a family of your own, and to think otherwise would be deluding yourself and unfair to the prospective child. If you're not ready, things come up, or you need to take a break as suggested then do so because a child is after all for LIFE. Not just for Christmas.

Chapter Five – Match Made and Miracles

It was now 2015. Our adoption profile and reports had been sent to panel for assessment. All the training had been done but there was a final visit from our social worker on a few very important things to we had to decide on.

"Have you thought about age? Boy or girl? Even siblings? What about a child with disabilities or health needs?"

Crikey. We had no idea. What a decision. A son? A daughter? We were also aware that older kids weren't chosen as often. Was that something we could take on? It's an awful feeling not wanting to say no to any of these options when you know there's potentially a child out there that needs you.

We were still young at this point, we had no parenting experience, let alone disability experience. We had only one spare room, which meant if we were to choose a sibling pair then they would need to be two girls or two boys only. What an amazing opportunity we could give by keeping them together for the rest of their lives! But two? Straight away? Reluctantly, we ticked the boxes (can you believe there are tick boxes for this!) that said no to older kids, no to siblings and no to disability or heath needs. I felt absolutely horrendous doing this and had to say a prayer of forgiveness to get the guilt off my chest. But you must be completely honest. Our social worker didn't judge us in the slightest but encouraged us to be realistic. We were told we had to be selfish in the choices we made, or we could potentially end up in a situation we weren't ready for. We were new kids on the block ourselves and we had to be true to our hearts. With everything being considered we decided we wanted as young a child as possible.

"What about foster to adopt?" she said.

We knew about foster to adopt obviously through our training, but we also saw the reality of it from close friends. Both good and bad. This is a completely different undertaking which is also a completely different road to adopting.

We badly wanted a baby, but babies don't usually get put up for adoption until they're at least toddler age because it takes time for their case to go through the courts. The baby stays with you (as potential adoptive parents) until the time comes when you can legally apply to adopt them. This can be wonderful in terms of attachment, less upheaval for the child and longevity for the future. But there is a potentially devastating downside which you need to be aware of. The baby has been taken from it's birth parent(s) for a reason. It may be birth mum is dealing with addiction, domestic violence or she's struggling to cope. Sometimes situations need time to fix/heal by where mum and baby can be reunited. If this actually happens and all is made right, then mum and baby should be together, but this can be very hard on the prospective adopters. There's no guarantee that the baby will be yours. Of course, every case is unique and may not have these issues in play. One such friend of ours did this and it was a clear-cut case, no chance of the child returning to its mother, so the process was fairly simple. But another, it was a whole year of trying to help mum and her desperate situation. They even did strict visitations with mum to help but it fell apart time and time again. Eventually after over a year of taking care of the little one, who was now almost a toddler, a new family member came forward to take the child for good. It was heart-breaking for everyone involved. Heart-breaking for the birth mother but also heart -

breaking for the family that took care of that child for so long. It takes a special kind of person(s) to be involved in this process and we knew pretty quickly, due to what we had been through over the last six years, we could not cope with a situation like this. So after plenty of discussions, we were in a position to excitedly say we would love to adopt a toddler and would be delighted with either a boy or a girl.

It was June, we got the call, our panel day was booked in. The final stage of our adoption application.

We were sat in front of a long table full of various professionals who shot fired questions at us about our report. It was no piece of cake! The only way to describe it is was like having a job interview with five or six people sat in front of you and you're taking an oral exam at the same time. I was terrified of saying anything wrong! I know my husband felt the same. Luckily, we could sit together and hold each other's hand during the interrogation. Good grief, these were the people that would decide if we could have a child or not. I really don't know how we did it. I know I didn't eat any breakfast that morning but as always, our

lovely social worker was there sat to one side –
smiling at us. It was ok, ten to fifteen minutes now
for the rest of our lives.

In front of us sat the head of the local authority,
head of child services, another social worker, a
child psychologist, and an adult adoptee. I'm sure
there was more, it certainly felt that way. I haven't
got the foggiest recollection what they asked us.
Complete blur. All I know is at the very end of,
what seemed to be endless scribbling of notes, they
smiled, thanked us for coming and we were sent to
a tiny waiting room down the corridor. It was done.
We waited. Time had never passed so slowly. The
head of children's services came through the door
and, with a big smile, asked us to come back to the
panel room. We sat back in the same seats before
the judges who announced we had unanimously
been approved!

"We even have a baby in mind" The head said.
"It's just perfect!".

We were elated and thanked everyone involved.

After a lot of hugs and phone calls to parents we
drove to the nearest nice pub to have a well-earned
drink and a slap-up lunch, due to my stomach going

back down to where it belonged and reminding me it hadn't been fed yet that day. We couldn't be happier and proceeded to message all our family and friends that we were officially approved adopters! Now we had to wait for THE call, the 'we have a child for you' call. And that call came, very quickly. We kind of sensed that would happen from what the gentleman said at panel. It was true. We had been matched with a baby boy who was six months old, and his papers were just going through court now. We were told confidentially why he was in care, but I will not divulge that information due to data protection. It was set in stone, there was no chance of baby returning to any family, his adoption was being finalised and they'd be in touch to let us know when we could go and meet him. A few weeks later another call came but it was not the news we were expecting. During the court proceedings a blood test had been carried out that revealed the father of the child was not who the mother had stated on his birth certificate. Now, due to legality, came the long task for the authorities to track down his true biological father. It was their absolute legal obligation to do this and rightly so, but that didn't make us feel any better. We felt very conflicted because although it was deeply upsetting for us, we wanted what was best for the little boy. The only comfort came from the fact we hadn't met him yet, didn't know his name or had even seen a picture. It was grace that it happened when it did rather than further down the line.

I still think about that little boy even now. I hope wherever he is, whatever his situation, that he's ok, happy, and loved.

A further revelation came from the authorities.

"Sorry but we don't have anything else from your criteria in the pipeline right now. In a few months we could try the national registry." We were deflated. We felt our dream had been ripped away from us just as it was about to get started. That six months break they suggested earlier, now sounded like a very good idea to us both.

Then I got sick, very sick. I couldn't eat anything; I couldn't keep anything down or even stay awake. I had to take time off work. Had the whole adoption process taken its toll on my health? Had I been exhausted by it all? The next month, August, I made an appointment to see my GP who suggested I see a specialist at the hospital on gastroenterology. He had no clue what was wrong with me but was very worried.

Then came the evening we ran out of cat food….! What!?! I hear you say…. Bear with me, it will become clear why I'm sharing this in a few moments. We had, at this time, two cats named Charlie and Lola (named by my little niece and nephew!) who, that evening yowled at us from the kitchen for their dinner only for us to look in the cupboard and find it empty. We took a quick trip to Asda.

"Babe, when are you due on next?" My husband said.

"I have no idea. In fact, I really don't know."

"Weren't you due on like two weeks ago?"

"No don't be silly I'll check on the calendar when I get home."

"I'm buying a pregnancy test just to make sure. You have been really sick lately"

"Are you joking!?"

And so, the conversation went on for quite some time about how we've not got pregnant in SEVEN years so why is tonight any different. He was insistent and grabbed the first response test. Whilst our chat continued, at that moment a work colleague of mine and her mother walked around the corner to see him place the test on top of the basket.

"Are you pregnant!?" she said instantly.

Instantly I wanted to run and hide somewhere or say rather sarcastically… "Yes, I'm pregnant that's why we're buying a test you numb skull!" But I'm not a rude person, so I lovingly replied in a whisper... "Don't tell anyone ok!"

They both grinned with absolute pleasure at being in on a secret that was so juicy. We left under the cover of darkness with the test and, of course, some cat food.

Reluctantly I went to the bathroom to pee on the stick.

After a few minutes I glanced at the test, expecting the usual one liner (at least I thought that's what you see when it's negative – I hadn't done one of these tests in almost two years). But there it was TWO big fat pink lines. I started to shake and had to hold the side of the wall to stop myself from passing out. I shouted for my husband. He was ecstatic! And we both cried. How did this happen? Is this true? Were we dreaming? I remember calling my mum in hysterics, not checking the time before hand, when she sleepily replied, "Are you sure?". Well, we thought that too. The very next day my husband bought every brand of pregnancy test going and had me pee on all of them. It was undeniable. Even the word 'pregnant' flashed over and over again on one of them. I called our GP immediately to tell him, he couldn't believe it either! Over the next few days, we were in total shock. Every person we told sobbed as much as we did. This journey had not been done alone. Our doctor arranged an early scan for me, just to be on the safe side given my complicated history. But there on the screen, heartbeat pumping away – was our baby. There SHE was! Looking back, we were quick off the mark to share our pregnancy news. It was still early on, but we had to let people know. Work needed an explanation for my sickness, family needed to know I was ok and the adoption agency…. Oh no… how were we going to tell them!? I still feel guilty about making that phone call. So much so, I made my husband do it. You're on the approved adopters list and you go and get yourself pregnant… I felt terrible. But it happens! More often than you realise! We certainly didn't think it would happen to us and we were so grateful for the way they responded.

"We are delighted for you. To be honest we were all devastated how our plans fell through for you and that there was nothing else immediately we could do. We couldn't be happier."

Now we had our peace. She came by divine intervention; she was meant to be here, and her timing could not have been more perfect.

Chapter Six – Blissful Blessing, Brutal Reality

Our amazing daughter arrived in May 2016 after I was induced on her due date. She has stopped growing on our last check up and they needed to get her out sooner rather than later. For me, being induced involved having a pessary of hormones put up in between my legs (lots more unpleasant when a baby is filling up the entire space). I know for some this can drag on, as it did for my own mother when she had me. IV drugs were needed to help speed things along.

After a long weekend wait at the hospital our baby girl decided to come after nine hours of contractions and 'can't quite remember' some very blurry minutes or hours of pushing. Gas and air did wonders for my focus, although all I could manage to say throughout was "water", whenever I needed to quench my thirst in between pushes. The only way to describe contractions is that it was like having a balloon inflate and deflate in your stomach at various different intervals. The quicker more frequent they come, the more it hurts. I knew it was time to push when the pain became unbearable. Too late for pain relief, she was coming. I climbed up on the bed and held onto the metal headframe.

"Push!" the midwife called out.

"Push how?" I replied.

"Just do a poo dear."

What!? Do a poo? Is she kidding? By this point I was in too much pain and remember thinking to myself 'screw it, I'm going to do a poo on this bed, in front of all of these people.' I was very pleased that at that moment my husband was NOT at the business end because I'm pretty sure that's exactly what I did next. Whatever, I was having a baby! I did this several more times until I could push no more.

*Can I just point out for those who may be facing labour for the first time, this is not continuous. You do get a 'breather' in between contractions but just not for as long as before. It's a little something to grasp for in the moment! *

"I think I'm going to die!" I said to the midwife very dramatically.

"That's because she's here. One last push, you've got this." Then I felt it, the ring of fire. A very lame example of this would be like how your bottom feels after relieving yourself from last night's extremely spicy curry – except it's your vagina. Her head was coming out and then comes that surreal feeling, when the baby comes completely out, and you feel like all your insides have fallen out with them. You feel as if your whole body has lost its skeletal form and you succumb to the exhaustion into a pool of mush. Your body spent.

But then you hear it…. that little whimper… and all the clean-up, stitching, poking and comings and goings carries on around you like a clouded reality as you hold this little miracle in your arms. I was in heaven, completely exhausted, but in heaven. I had literally been given a gift from above and she was ours. I still can't believe it to this day, after ALL those years of waiting and trying. My heart bursts every moment with gratitude and thankfulness.

I had it easy where pregnancies and birth are concerned. Apart from the first three months of intense sickness and nausea, the rest of my pregnancy was a breeze. The birth was very straight forward, and I had her naturally with no problems. I feel incredibly privileged to have had that experience because so many women do not.

There is so much unknown, so much uncertainty, and tragically so much that could go wrong. Thankfully, for me it all went well.

Then came the next few weeks of family, friends, colleagues all popping over with gifts, food, and cuddles. If you're fortunate, your partner gets a couple of weeks off with you to adjust to your new life. Then after that week or two – 'kablam' you're at home, alone with this tiny human being that solely depends on you knowing what you're doing and can keep up with it. This is where brutal reality kicked in for me, but it wasn't until months down the line that things really came crashing down and my world wasn't the same. Another privilege I got to experience with my daughter was that of breastfeeding. I was so lucky that for me, this too came easily for the both of us. She had no problem latching on and, once we got our positions worked out, she would happily feed, and it felt wonderful. But it didn't feel wonderful when it happened every TWO HOURS …. Night AND day! Looking back, I wish I had got my daughter used to a bottle, even if it was just for some of the of the time so my husband could do some of her feeds. But the concept from midwives and society of 'breast is best' became a very damaging statement for me.

Yes, breast milk is the best option for your baby for many reasons but sometimes this is not an option for mothers and for some, like me, feel demonised for even thinking of not pushing through the woes of breastfeeding. Shouldn't there also be a supporting statement that comes with this?... 'healthy mother is best?' My opinion at that time was, I wanted this baby so much, I'm her mother, I need to give her what's best and that's my milk. However, I was slowly destroying myself. I was getting absolutely no solid sleep, an hour here an hour there. I was like a zombie and I somehow kept this up for EIGHT months before I finally collapsed. Can you imagine was it's like? … Eight months of being woken every two hours in the night and then being needed again with that same frequency throughout the day. Being a mother puts you on high alert with any noise day or night and if you're on your own during the daytime, proper naps were also out of the question. What does that do to your mind and body!? My physicality suffered, I had dropped down to six and a half stone by the time she was seven months old, and my mental health was in pieces. My husband did say at one point, "I think you need to give some of the feeding responsibilities to daddy," but she wouldn't take to a bottle and my poor hubby didn't know what to do next to support me. On the other hand, if anyone else had dared suggest that to me, I would have been horrified and said no. Again, she was my baby, the one I wanted for so long, I'm her mother no one else, she needs me and my milk. In the process I began to resent breastfeeding. My body was not my own and neither was my mind. I hate writing this part of our journey, but I believe it's essential to share since, I know, there's so many women out there who are struggling with the after effects of having a baby and I want you to know – although we are all very different our experiences can overlap and we need to look out for each other.

At work, and home, I love listening to Radio 2. The only snag is when 12 o'clock hits with Jeremy Vine, the tunes stop, and the people ring in for what me and my colleagues call 'the whingeing hour.' Sorry Jeremy, nothing personal! But one particular morning, during writing this book in 2022, I left it running and the subject matter was announced 'The Baby Blues. Is it just the blues or something more sinister?' My ears pricked up. I was interested to hear what was being put forward. Jeremy, alongside a female doctor, and the general public joined in on the discussion. The 'blues' (feeling low, down or generally not yourself) normally occurs after you've had a baby and can last up to thirteen weeks. This is considered normal as your body and hormones adjust themselves after birth -it usually passes with no issues. However, there is a more serious post-natal depression that can hit months down the line that sometimes women don't expect or understand. Sometimes this can, for some rare individuals, progress or come in the form of psychosis and needs it be addressed immediately.

A brave young woman rang in to share her story about having had twins around nine months ago, one had tragically passed away not long after the birth. She was able to face that loss with much help and support, however, her other child was now months old, and she wasn't coping. She knew she wasn't herself and also knew it wasn't grief. She had lost all her joy; she didn't know how-to carry-on day to day and was scared why she was feeing this way. She explained, when she had lost her other child, the help came flooding in immediately from healthcare professionals, family, friends etc etc (Absolutely rightly so! No one under any circumstance should have to face the unbearable loss of their child, especially alone.) She was able to access the correct counselling and support she needed without having to search for it herself. But here she was now, months later, deeply struggling. Yet when she reached out for help from people she trusted she got responses like,

"You've got this beautiful baby that's healthy, why are you so depressed?"

"What have you got to be sad about? All is well. Enjoy your miracle."

The doctor on the radio was fantastic. So gentle, kind and supportive. She explained that, indeed PND can hit months down the line for some women and professionals are not too sure why. Of course, there can be contributing factors like lifestyle, family inheritance and general mental health conditions that can make this more likely. Upon gently enquiring some more of this ladies' situation she said,

"Me and my husband had a lot of fertility issues and waited and tried for a long time before our children came along."

It sounded like I was hearing parts of myself from four years ago. Then the doctor then said something new, something that in all my reading and research on fertility I hadn't heard before. Women who face issues when trying to conceive can be up to 20% more likely to suffer PND than those who don't. However, much more research needs to be done on this and, as I've said before, each women's experience is individual and needs to be assessed that way to confirm if other factors are leading to PND. I will elaborate more on this by sharing more on this part of my journey…

One weekend, there was an intervention. My wonderful husband could tell I was in a bad way and recognised the endless feeds were destroying me – we needed to get our daughter on a bottle. My mother and mother-in-law came round to support him whilst I went upstairs, away from her sight and smell, to spend the weekend in bed. After six to eight hours, from what I can remember of that day, for the first time ever she miraculously accepted the formula and had feeds with her daddy no problem. At this point you'd think I would be shouting for joy, shouting from the rooftops – absolutely not– I felt like a complete failure. The most important task in life of being a mother and I had fallen at the first hurdle. After that weekend, when my husband returned to work, I hit rock bottom. What was the reason I was here? To be a good mum. I wasn't breastfeeding her anymore and my exhaustion from sleepless days and nights had left me completely agoraphobic and a hollow shell of my former self. Don't get me started on the panic attacks.

I couldn't attend baby groups. They were too much for me. I couldn't handle seeing other mothers having it 'easy', saying how their baby has slept through since birth and all the exciting plans they had for that week (I also came off all social media for the very same reason.) I know some of it was a front but even so, I couldn't face that environment and that became another way to beat myself up, because I felt my daughter was missing out on important interaction with other children. Anxiety, depression, hopelessness became my existence. That day I looked at my daughter and said to her "You'd be better off without me. You have a family who love you so much, a daddy who'd take amazing care of you. You don't need a mother who doesn't feed you breastmilk anymore, who's always miserable, who can't even leave the house and who's so tired she has no energy to properly play with you." That day I truly wanted to end my life. But I didn't want to do anything whilst I was alone with her, I couldn't, I wouldn't. She was and is my everything. I needed to know she was always safe before I left this world. I considered taking a lone drive that evening but, in God's divine timing, my husband came home early that afternoon to find me sat on the living room floor, staring into oblivion, drenched in my tears. He gently sat beside me and held me. He knew it was really bad. I told him everything in that moment, I told him I wanted to die.

**I'm absolutely sobbing right now recalling these words for you. It's a disconcerting feeling looking back on yourself and your own heart breaks for your past situation. I can still feel that pain, I completely understand why I felt that way, but I'm completely separated from it now and I'm so grateful I didn't act on my desperation. I beg of you, if you're feeling this way or know someone who is please get help immediately. Call a family member you trust, a friend, your GP or a helpline charity (See the back of this book for examples). Be completely honest, do not be ashamed in any way because I promise you things WILL get better, and this can be the start of that for you. **

My husband called my GP straight away and we were given an emergency appointment to see him. I told him everything. This was essential, absolutely imperative.

"Look at your daughter." He said to me.

"She is a beautiful, healthy, happy little girl and YOU did that. You've done amazing. Can you see?" He was right. I had also been suffering body dysmorphia with regards to my daughter, I saw her as wasting away because my milk wasn't enough and that's why she was feeding so often. Having an outsider say those words to me changed my outlook but I was no where near ok.

"We're going to put you on some antidepressants to ease your PND and get you some help from the health visitors, ok?"

Can I just say – my husband and GP saved my life that day. If it wasn't for their care, observations, and quick responses I believe I wouldn't be here.

The two weeks that followed involved daily/ alternate day visits from my heath visitor, who was wonderful. She would stay and chat with me, play with my daughter and genuinely cared about my wellbeing. Each day she would affirm me, build my self-confidence, and help me to look forward. Along with the medication, more rest and recovery

I started to feel like myself again. I also attended some CBT (Cognitive behavioural therapy) groups once a week to try and teach me, and other families, how to re-focus our thinking from negativity and try to give us life skills to deal with anxiety and panic attacks. For me, the groups didn't help. Hearing other people's personal problems at this point only made me feel worse. Although this kind of group therapy didn't work for me it does work for others, I know because I've seen it. It can be exactly what other parents need.

I finally realised my true problem was just exhaustion. I had pushed myself so hard to be the perfect providing mother and, in the process, I had neglected myself and all I needed right now was some form of recovery. Once my daughter was in a routine with the bottles, I allowed my husband to share the feeding responsibilities. She napped the same time each day so I could begin having proper rest and night-time sleeps became longer – I felt like a new person. I got my appetite back; I got my energy back and I got my confidence back. I could think straight again, my emotions levelled out and I could feel joy again. Perhaps, if had had a baby that slept more since day one, I may not have had such a traumatic experience with PND. I had already suffered with some anxiety before my daughter came along, so had this experience acerbated this? Perhaps, perhaps not. Did the medication really help? Perhaps, perhaps not. Either way, with all the help and support that was put into place for me both practically and emotionally I felt I had my feet back on the floor again. I came off the tablets, went back to work part time and started living again. I've come to realise when I'm having a bad day emotionally, distraction is sometimes the best thing for me (although this may not be that case for others) so going back to work for me was a God send. Please let me reiterate that my experience is my own. I know that there are mothers out there who's PND could be rectified with the correct medication, the invaluable and important therapy sessions or just the care of others. All these things individually and collectively can-do wonders. I urge you, if you're struggling, please don't suffer alone. Seek these things out to get the help you need. Don't let it be an acceptance of failure, let it be an acceptance of help for a new beginning and the sun WILL shine once again for you.

Chapter Seven – One, Two, Third time lucky?

After a year or two of adjusting to being a working mother and feeling back to myself again as much as possible. We started talking about having another baby. I'd had the experience now of pregnancy, gone through childbirth and learnt valuable lessons on bringing up a baby being acutely aware of my own heath at the same time – and I felt sure I could do it again. Although we continued to talk about a sibling for our daughter, we didn't actually give it a serious thought until May 2019.

I hadn't been feeling all too well but things took a strange turn when I attended a family birthday party. During that afternoon I experienced the most awful pains in my womb. It felt like (what I can only imagine!) a sharp knife had been stuck into me in one specific spot. It took my breath away and nearly made me pass out. I don't quite remember what happened the rest of that day but, I guess as a lot of women do, I just carried on not sure what it was or what to do. It was when I went to work the next day things got worse. Again, I felt very poorly all day and then at the end (thankfully!) of my shift I started to bleed. I thought 'oh well, auntie flow is here' but this time it was very different. The pain was intense, and I couldn't stop bleeding – it was literally pouring out of me. I was scared stiff. I knew it wasn't my usual experience of the 'mensises' (women know what their normal periods are like!). I remember driving home, putting all my concentration on getting home safely, and then running across the road with blood dripping out the bottom of my trouser legs across the road to my front door. When I got through the door, I didn't do my usual 'Hi everyone!' I ran straight upstairs to the bathroom and sat on the loo so I could bleed without making any mess or causing distress for anyone else (crazy statement I know! But that's how I think!). Once again, my gallant husband rung our doctor's surgery and got a call back from our GP.

"Is there any chance you were pregnant?" She asked me.

I was totally taken aback.

"Yes, I guess it's totally possible. I was late but I hadn't taken a test. I hadn't crossed my mind because of our history."

After a longer chat about my symptoms from the day previous, checking on how I was doing at that moment and ruling other things out she said,

"I believe you're having a miscarriage. I am so sorry"

I was in shock. That word had never been on my radar. I was someone who they thought couldn't have babies, not someone who lost them. I had no idea how to feel. I was now mourning something I never knew I had. You suddenly start to think, 'If I had known. Could I have saved it? Did I do something wrong?' The truth is – absolutely not. It happens far too often, 1 in 4 is the statistic, especially so early on in a pregnancy and now I was acutely aware I was part of those numbers. It was over before it had even begun and now my longing for another child grew stronger.

That summer, we properly began trying for a baby. Not as 'proper' as I've done (future me speaking here) but I'll explain that later. At this point I'm talking about keeping an accurate track on my periods and knowing my fertile days. This is usually on days 10-16 of your cycle depending on if you're regular or not. Ovulations tests can really help and pinpoint these days for you if it's something you need a little help with. Amazingly, to our disbelief we did indeed fall pregnant again and this time we did do a test to confirm and got the all-important second line. We were delighted but, reacted completely differently to when we found out we were expecting our daughter. We remained slightly reserved and mindful that not all things go well at the start. I'm so sad to write that for us, the second time round it didn't. I knew it when a few days later I had that same sharp pain and as I laid painfully over the kitchen sink, it all came to an end.

Warning – graphic description of miscarriage

As I began to lightly bleed, I sat on the toilet, expecting it to be like before but then I heard something drop into the basin. There in the water was the tiniest gestational sac, only as big as a pea. I looked and saw nothing inside it but a mix of colours. I knew in that moment, that had been that start of my growing baby and for whatever reason it couldn't grow any further and had been expelled from my body.

Graphic over

I was heartbroken, but not lost. I had only been around four weeks or so along. It was very early days and I'm certain that my baby had never made it to a stage of significant development, especially since I had 'seen' that with my own eyes. Either my little one was poorly, or the chromosomes didn't fit together, my body knew that and ended things as they had begun to come together.

I needed to think this way to compartmentalise our loss, to know our child hadn't yet reached a form of consciousness therefore had not felt any pain or suffering. Nevertheless, it didn't take away the fact we had just lost a baby. It was another hard time for us but, strangely, although we were very upset, we had peace and were thankful it happened early on.

Life happened as it does and in the early part of 2020, other matters took precedence, and I had an operation to have my tonsils removed. I was ALWAYS getting tonsilitis and eventually gave in to pay for the procedure privately since the NHS demanded I have it at least SEVEN times in a row to even be considered for a tonsillectomy. It was either be on antibiotics for life (which the specialist suggested – stupid idea!) or I lose my job from being off sick so much. I wasn't prepared to do either. The operation itself is fine but it's a horrible recovery period afterwards and I won't put you through my experience of that today! But once that time had passed, I felt like a new woman and consequently, it seems, fell pregnant! We were ecstatic to be expecting again after all the years of infertility beforehand and all the problems we had gone through. We had also just started building an extension onto our house (we were the typical Grand Design family – start a big project, spend lots of money and get yourself pregnant!) The future was looking bright, we made a conscious choice to be positive and enjoy being on cloud nine. The weeks ticked by, it was spring time, all the lambs were being born in the fields across from our house, the sunshine was warming, the daffodils were in bloom, my daughter had started school and was loving it and then…. Boom… COVID LOCKDOWN. I'm not going to talk about that, nobody wants to talk about that. I was classed as an essential worker so carried on as normal, with the fun of home schooling around it, and my husband was furloughed. My work decided to put me on leave after a while due to concerns around me catching covid and the risks potentially to my pregnancy. Thank goodness that happened when it did because I needed to be at home as on one particular sunny Friday morning, I found blood in my pants. It was not a lot but enough to make both me and my husband afraid. I called my GP who knew my history and arranged an emergency scan for me. I was terrified. Not again I thought. I had no idea what to expect this time, I had no pain, I was much further along than ever before, and we were also in a global pandemic! This 'little' problem meant my husband couldn't go to the hospital with me – for anything! It was a horrendous time for the world but for also very much so for us also, just for a very different reason. What if I got bad news? What if I had to stay in the hospital? Would I be alone? Could I do this? I shouldn't have to be thinking these things!!

"There's your baby." The sonographer said. "And I'm sure you want to see the heart beating."

I can't explain that feeling of relief and gratitude. It was overwhelming and I burst into tears. "Ba boom, Ba boom."

"Your babies got a strong heartbeat. Everything is fine. You can get excited now and start planning." I was discharged from the hospital with the all clear and, as I waited for my scan pictures, a friend of mine (who works there as a midwife) spotted me and saw my tearful flushed face.

"It'll all be fine." She reassured me. "Once you have a healthy heartbeat, the chance of loss falls to around 6% or even lower." I was elated. I walked out of that hospital the happiest woman on the planet, clutching my scan pictures and my little baby bump. My husband was wating for me at the top of the stairs with my daughter, who knew I was pregnant, already crying.

"Everything's fine babe." I said, hugging him on the floor. I'll never forget him collapsing from relief. It was a hugely emotional moment. I knew he felt helpless not being able to be by my side at the ultrasound and was gutted that he wasn't able to see our baby on the screen with its heart beating away beautifully. But he rested on the dream and excitement that in around six months' or so time he would be holding our new little one.

Chapter Eight – When it all comes crashing down...

End of May 2020. I remember it like it was yesterday. My bleeding had restarted again, but it was a weekend. Luckily, I had the phone number to the maternity unit at the hospital, so I gave them a call.

"A little bleeding is ok, I'm sure everything is fine. You had a recent scan."

"Yes, but I'm really worried." I said.

"I'm sure it's alright. Just give it a day or two and if by Tuesday your sill bleeding come in to see us. In the meantime, if it gets worse and you're in a lot of pain, go to A&E and they will refer you to us, but you must come ALONE."

Ok I thought, don't panic. However, over the course of the next few days the bleeding did not stop but I was no having bad cramps. I just knew something was wrong, but I didn't want to admit it. I don't know why I did what I did next, divine guidance maybe, but I began to research everything I could on what to expect with a miscarriage at my stage of pregnancy. I was just coming to three months (the supposed safe zone!?) the baby was alive and growing well in my womb – what the heck was going to happen if it all went wrong!?

This is what baffles me. At no point in my life, or any other woman's life that I know of are you taught or informed about miscarriages. You're given lesson on taking responsibility for your own sexual health, the ins and outs of periods and, of course, all about pregnancy. But at no stage are you told what to look out for or what to expect when things don't work out. It is not included in any sexual health curriculum in any schools or educational settings at this time.

There is such a thing as 'missed' miscarriage, when you carry on with your pregnancy, have your first scan at around ten to twelve weeks to then be told your baby hasn't developed and there's no heartbeat. Sometimes there will be a gestational sac but it's empty or the there's actually nothing to be seen on the screen as your body may have reabsorbed the embryo after a quick loss. Your baby has gone but your hormones still tell you are pregnant. Not only is that absolutely devastating news for the parents but you may be faced with the decision of either having the baby surgically removed (if there is still a little one present) or be given medication to take at home which, unaided, you are left for your body to expel the embryo naturally.

One of my friends had this situation thrust upon her. At the scan she was told the sad news that the baby had never lived and was straight away asked what she wanted to do. She told me she just went along with the surgery (called a D&C) never really given a second to process what had just happened, let alone to grieve. Can you imagine what that's like? Put yourself in her shoes. You're healthy, happy, going along thinking your baby is well and growing only to find out at the health scan, that at some point recently your baby didn't make it and now you have to face the fact of death rather than life…. I know this is not the case for everyone but when she told me all this, I couldn't help but cry along with her. Her words were, "I felt like a conveyor belt." After the surgery she was asked, "What do you want to do with the tissue?" The TISSUE!? For goodness sake. I don't know if my friends nurse was trying to disconnect from the situation but to use a medical term like that to describe someone's baby, in my opinion, is disgusting. Our tears continued to flow together the more she shared with me. She was asked if she wanted it cremated or to take it home to bury herself.

Can I just stop here. For a woman who has never had a miscarriage or faced a loss in this way, this is a truly horrific question to be asked flippantly. The sudden realisation that you have just lost your child and now in the space of a few hours you've gone from expecting a normal pregnancy scan to now having to decide what to do with your child's remains… It's unbearable. Especially for those who must face this further down the line. If you are a nurse, a midwife, or any healthcare professional I beg you, please remember each patient is an individual. Yes, it is unfortunately common, yes you may see this day in day out but no matter the circumstances that woman has lost her baby who she has loved the minute she saw those two lines. Please grieve with them, give the time they need to process what is happening and recognise the life that has been lost, no matter how small.

I knew I was losing my baby that day in 2020, so I wanted to know everything that was going to happen, how it would happen and when so I could take charge of the situation and do it in my own time and space. I googled everything! Even the aspects of miscarriage I didn't want to know or see because it saved me the future shock. I asked google images what a three-month miscarriage 'looks' like. Not just the quantity of blood but what my baby would actually look like at this stage if it came out now. I know for some of you this maybe too much but, for me and my own sanity, I wanted to prepare myself and not lose my head when I know it was going to happen. The world was going through a global pandemic, there was no cure, people were dying and there was no way I was going into A&E unless it was 100% necessary for me to do so. But one evening I felt tremendous pain and it got worser. I found myself breathing through cramps like I did when I was in the early stages of labour with my daughter. It revved up and I found myself clutching my womb praying to God through my sobbing, begging him 'please make it stop,' I knew that was it, I knew my baby was gone and I knew if I called an ambulance there was nothing they could do/give me to stop this happening. And there was no way I was going to the hospital, by myself without my husband! I just wanted the pain to stop and for it to all be over with because it was all too much.

Warning Graphic description

In my pain, and in a moment of clarity, I sat up on my knees. Then I felt it. Like the inside of my womb had slipped out into my underwear. I could feel the heat between my legs. I ran to the bathroom in hysterics and took off my pants to find it filled with a huge blood clot filling up the entire space of my knickers. To describe it better, it looked like someone had put an adult liver in my pants. I expected this because I had googled it. I knew my child was in there, so I broke apart the tissue and found nestled amongst the bloody mess was my beautiful little baby. My perfect baby still snugged inside the gestational sac, floating like an angel in the fluid. Our baby was amazing, no bigger than the palm of my hand (and I have small hands). Beautiful eyes, nose, mouth, hands, legs, and feet. Its little legs were still fused together, and the toes hadn't yet fully formed and separated. You know in the book 'what to expect when you're expecting' and they have an illustration at the start of each week to show what your babby looks like at that stage…ours looked exactly as expected. In my head, when you're pregnant there's still that disconnection because you can't really 'see' what your child looks like as they're growing, you never see them developing with your own eyes. Ultrasounds, although amazing, don't give you a clear picture of features and size. Unless you're further along and are privileged to have a 3D scan, otherwise you have to guess and imagine it all in your mind until the day your baby is born. But here I was in my bathroom holding my baby still in its sac within my hands. I could not love that baby more if I tried. My husband came into the bathroom.

"I'm sorry." I sobbed.

"Have we lost the baby?" he asked.

"Yes" I said. "Do you want to see our baby?" I could tell from the look on his face he was not expecting me to say that. Again, men are taught to a degree about women's health, periods, and pregnancy but they too are not educated on miscarriages and, at different stages, what that really involves. He held our baby too, crying.

"It's not your fault. Don't ever think that." He said. I knew it wasn't but, in that moment, I felt my world had come crashing down and my body had failed me. I wanted to hold our baby forever, I wanted to put it back in and pretend its heart would start beating again and everything would be alright. My perfect little baby. We decided not to break open the gestational sac in case it caused any damage or disfigurements. We found a small box, wrapped it carefully and placed it in the freezer. Because of this, and babies' stage of development, we never knew if it was a boy or a girl, so privately we called our little one Sammy. Although I still ache about the not knowing for sure on the sex of our baby, our local hospital didn't offer testing at this point anyway so it wouldn't have changed anything. Regardless, our baby was ours, will always be ours and I will forever be a mummy to a heavenly angel. I rang the hospital to tell them what had happened. I'm sorry to say there was no sympathetic ear from the other end of the phone that day, no sorrow, no empathy, not even an enquiry to my state of health or mind. I was given the same two options that my friend had been given when she lost baby. Bluntly, with no emotion.

"You can bring it to the hospital to be cremated or you can bury it at home – just don't put it near a water source."

What the heck!? I know you need to say these things but for crying out loud, the know the circle of life is common for some professions but it isn't necessarily for the patient! Learn to sympathise with individuals! Why else would I call for guidance!? And don't ever call my baby, or anyone else's baby for that matter, an IT!!

Graphic description ended

Adding insult to injury we found out that the government were living a double life behind our backs. Whilst I was at home in desperate grief (as were so many others in the world because of losses through covid) we were told that under no circumstances should we mix with people, stay at home, do not visit each other in different settings, so not to spread the horrendous virus that was then terrorising the nations. Here I was being an upright citizen, even at the worst stage of my life, desperate to be with my own mother for comfort, I did what the leaders of our country told me to do. Yet, we later found out, the prime mister and his 'cronies' were holding wine and cheese parties, getting drunk, falling over each other and bragging about breaking the rules. I wouldn't want to be Boris Johnson if he should ever run into my husband. He never got to see our baby alive on the ultrasound, he never got the opportunity to attend any appointments or be by my side at various consultations and tests. He did what he believed everyone else was doing to protect every single equally important individual. But we were so cruelly mistaken. This is when my belief in God was actually made stronger because he promises to bring vengeance on these kinds of heartless people. When we feel so powerless and cannot direct our anger in the manner we want to, he promises to do it for us. I know, one day, they will have the creator to answer to and that is the only consolations for such selfish behaviour from those whom you trust. Forgiveness can only be given by God for those individuals (if they truly regret their actions) because it certainly won't come from me. Perhaps in time I will soften but right now, I have to push it out of my mind and heart for my own sanity.

During the extensive preparation reading on google I did, the other information I came across was aftercare. I phoned the hospital after everything had happened and said...

"Shouldn't I have a scan? Don't you need to check I'm ok?" I really pushed for this because, surely, I had just been through a major trauma and shouldn't someone, like a medical professional at least, check everything is alright? Thank God I did because after having a scan the following day, the found I still had the placenta stuck in my womb. If you've suffered a miscarriage, absolutely tell your GP or Women's hospital. Discuss with them what has happened, how far along you were and they can support you in getting the correct care. But also, be informed as much as you can handle so that certain stages of that care are not overlooked or missed. This is the very reason I am writing this book, so that my experiences can guide and help those of you (or if you know of someone) who are facing these awful situations without guidance and knowing the safest place to get experienced knowledge. I still can't believe that after asking the midwife on duty about my aftercare, her response was 'Yea I suppose if you want to.' I admit it seems my journey is riddled with negativity and I'm sure that, or I'd certainly hope that most women's hospitals don't react this way and their care is what it should be. At least me telling my story can help and prepare others if they don't get the right treatment they're entitled to.

Because of the covid pandemic, the midwives were very reluctant to admit me. I had to sit in the waiting room, alone, nervously thinking about what would come next. How I wish my husband was with me because the emotional turmoil that came that day was terrible for me. For the love of everything sacred, I wish women's hospitals would have separate waiting rooms because I had to sit there for the next half an hour listening to other women cooing over their scan pictures, asking excited questions, and talking about their future plans. I wanted to burst into to tears and run as fast as I could out of that place. Those women had no idea, just the day before, my baby had died and, although I had a bump and was in a maternity ward, there wasn't going to be a child coming in a few months' time. I was grieving, they were celebrating. Those two emotions should NOT be put together. It's unbelievably cruel.

The midwife called me to the office and said I had three options. I could have an operation to remove what was left (again, a D&C, as explained previously), I could go home with medication to help get it all out quicker or I could wait it out and see if it all came out naturally. I decided on option number three. I did NOT want to go through an operation without anyone by my side or at least visit me. I didn't want the medication. I knew that option came with a significant amount of pain and I'd had enough pain to last me a lifetime. So to wait and take some time out for me was a sensible option and what I needed mentally too. They booked me in for another scan the following week to see how things were going. Because, after that time if things had still not passed, I would have to have the operation regardless to protect me from complications. The midwife I saw that day was an angel in uniform. She couldn't have been more sympathetic, gentle, and caring. She saw on my notes this was my third loss.

"I think it might be worth you having some tests to see if something is causing your miscarriages. Contact your GP when you're ready ok. In the meantime, if you fall pregnant again, speak to your GP about trying out something called progesterone pessaries and get yourself in for an early scan. But maybe give your body at least a month to heal and get back to some normality. Also, if you need some counselling, here are some great organisations to contact ok."

God bless that midwife. She was so attentive, I finally felt heard, someone was taking my individual experience seriously and tried to support me. It just goes to show, those professionals you come into contact with are also individuals and can affect the outcome of your journey. Some terrible, some amazing. Either way it shapes you. That day this wonderful midwife had also given me something new I was expecting – HOPE. Being in the medical profession I knew what she meant about the pessaries. Progesterone is given to help support the growth of the lining of your womb, the growing pregnancy and levels out hormones. It very typically to have this given to you before you start IVF. It's never a guarantee but it was something I could 'do' should I fall pregnant again and that feeling was empowering.

In the meantime, I did pass the placenta naturally. I took time off work to grieve, to rest bodily and to process and refocus my thoughts and emotions. We abstained for a month and decided not to try again until we had the tests done to see if anything came of them. After a time, I returned to work, which for me was a blessing. There is nothing like a bit of healthy distraction to help you feel yourself again but, more importantly, also to have understanding loving people by your side. I have worked with my colleagues for fifteen long years, it almost feels like a second home to me at times and I am part of the furniture! They were so gentle, kind, and compassionate. The first day back after my 'lockdown' miscarriage was extremely hard emotionally but they listened, held me when I cried and even grieved with me. This meant the world to me and made the transition back to work amazingly easy.

I contacted my GP and she agreed completely agreed in putting me forward for some tests. These would be;

1) Vaginal ultrasound – to check for growths, menstrual conditions (e.g., Fibroids) and the shape of my womb and cervix.

2) Antiphosphdipid (apl) antibody test – done by blood test to see if you have antibodies that may reject a pregnancy.

3) Lupus Anticoagulant test – done by blood tests to see if you have a blood clotting disorder that changes blood supply to the baby/placenta of which can cause miscarriage.

You may be also offered something called 'Karyotyping' which, if you've lost three babies, the foetus can be tested for chromosomal/DNA abnormalities.

This was not offered to me as our local area did not have the facility for this.

These were booked in for me. The blood tests were done at my GP surgery and the ultrasound at a smaller local hospital. The results would be given to me in three months' time at a consultant's meeting with a gynaecology specialist.

I urge you, if you've experienced multiple losses, please don't hesitate to get these tests. If you have a blood clotting issue it can be a simple as taking aspirin or blood thinners to carry your baby to full term, but you must speak with your GP first. If it's the path you want to take, then please don't wait, as simple intervention could change everything for you and your future family.

In response to our next options and the tests that were available to us we decided to do the only thing we could do together as a family during that time, we buried our baby at home. Our daughter got to see 'Sammy' and together we cried, said our goodbyes and 'love you's' before we placed our heavenly baby under our cherry blossom tree. Now each year when it blossoms, we think of our baby that, we believe, was too poorly for this world. I will always be a mother to a heavenly child. And the poem that reads underneath the tree's leaves will forever be true…

'Our hearts still ache with sadness

And secret tears still flow

What it meant to lose you

No one will ever truly know.

Until we meet again in heaven.'

Chapter Nine – Tests, tests and What now?

After losing our third baby, especially after each one getting further along each time, it had left me terrified of getting pregnant again. But I was left with the question – how did this all happen? A decade ago, we were facing YEARS of unexplained infertility and now after miraculously having our daughter we were dealing with unexplained re-occurrent miscarriages. I'd gone from not being able to get pregnant to being able to fall pregnant but not being able to keep them. Why? After a month's complete rest, I had the ultrasound which revealed no immediate issues. I then had TWELVE vials of blood taken at my surgery (make sure you take some sweets with you for that appointment – it's a life saver afterwards! My choice was Haribo strawberry laces – Yum!) and these were sent off to the lab to check for the various conditions. Those three months of waiting for the results, knowing they'd actually be ready at the doctor's surgery in approximately two weeks' time, felt insanely long and at times excruciating. But no, we had to wait for a specialist to go through them me – not us – because, of course, my husband still couldn't attend a single appointment to support me because of covid restrictions. In hindsight I was glad of the wait. It meant not jumping into another potential pregnancy loss which we were no way ready for. In the meantime, emotionally I was spiralling. Our baby's due date had come and gone. Others close to us were having healthy babies born when ours was meant to be with us and others were telling us they were expecting again. The strange thing is I could be happy for first time mothers. I was thrilled for them and shared in their joy but for those who were having their second or third I resented immensely. I was very much still grieving, and I was angry. I could not have wanted a baby more if I tried. I ached painfully for my child. I know to extent I always will. The problem with going through years of infertility makes you incredibly vulnerable emotionally about children in general. You appreciate them so much more in a way other's don't understand. My daughter is my everything and therefore any pregnancy I've had, I feel the same way towards them. To help process some of my feelings (particularly separation), me and my husband got tattoos. His was beautifully artistic. A mother, father and baby bird on a branch looking up to the clouds parting as a baby bird flies through the sun's rays to heaven. I sobbed when the tattooist showed me his sketch. The artist had gone well beyond the original brief and we were so thankful for his attentive creativity. I had a simple design of what our baby looked like. That way I felt my child was always with me and I'd never be without them.

There's a brilliant line in the last Hobbit film that sums up very simply what miscarriage (and other) loss feels like ...

"If this is love, why does it hurt so much?"

– Tauriel

"Because it was real." - Gandalf

On the morning of my results appointment, I got a phone call to say the specialist had an emergency and needed to reschedule for another time.

"Right" I said. "When will that be?" I asked. The young girl on the other end of the phone, poor love, I could hear the reluctance in her voice said. "Three months' time." I exploded.

"Seriously!? I'm sorry I know it's not your fault, but I've already waited three months for these results – can't I just be told them over the phone? Surely, I don't need to wait and come in? Can't you just tell me if I'm clear or not?"

"I'm sorry but I think it's better someone's goes through these with you."

Oh no. I thought. There's bad news. They've found something. So, I agreed to the next available appointment. But those extra months of waiting made my emotions even worse. All my anger and pain became directed at one person. They could have healthy planned pregnancies whenever they choose to. Was there any effort on their part? Why can't nature share the wealth? Why so many for some and not for others? I HATED her. (If you knew me, that is completely the opposite of my normal personality.) I knew it was completely irrational and unfair for me to think this way, so I sought out counselling from a long-term friend who knew my history and what it was like to face fertility issues.

"How do I deal with this?" I asked her desperately.

"Pray." She replied. "Tell God how you feel. Talk honestly with your husband. Stay away from situations you know that will trigger you, at least for a while. Baby showers, certain family gatherings or gender reveals. Etc. But if your feelings become all-consuming you MUST get professional help."

She was right. I told God I hated him, he's a big guy and knows my heart. He can handle me telling him my pain and how life is unfair, how he's unfair for giving and taking life and we have no understanding as to why. I told my husband I hated this woman; I was afraid of myself because it wasn't me, it was the pain talking and he told me to get help. He knew me and knew I had to allow myself to be angry for a time and I would be alright. But I refused professional counselling. I wasn't ready to help myself, I was revelling in my anger, it made me feel strong at a time when I felt weak and entirely unhinged.

The results appointment came round just before Christmas, I was terrified. I attended, unwillingly alone, for the specialist to sit down with me and tell me... I was completely fine. Silence. Seriously!? I waited SIX months to be told I'm negative for everything. I was fuming.

"So, I don't need any more care? There's no help or advice you can give me?" I asked.

"No." She said. "You'll be alright and I'm sure next time you'll have a healthy pregnancy. Thanks for coming in"

I was utterly flummoxed. Surely something had to be wrong. Surely you can give me some advice, you're a specialist for crying out. No mention of the pessary treatment the midwife suggested previously, no early scan offers or even an enquiry into my wellbeing and if I needed any mental health support. It was a ten second appointment. I felt invisible. She took a look at the computer screen, read out the results and then stared at me, silent, expecting me to just leave her office. I wanted to punch her for being so flippant and dismissive. Yes, I'm healthy, I'm grateful for that but put yourself in my shoes, I'm lost here. I left in a daze, sat in my car and sobbed. I wanted to drive my car into the wall that day. Yet again, no answers, no sympathy and no direction. Those same thoughts whispered in my head again from when I had PND. 'Everyone's better off without you, you're useless." But then I remembered the amazing family I had back at home. My wonderful supportive husband, my miracle beautiful daughter waiting to embrace me with love as soon as I walked through the door. I knew they'd understand my feelings.

For those of you out there supporting someone with fertility issues, never say 'It's good news you're healthy.' It's so strange I know but it's not what you want to hear. You pretty much want the specialists to find something wrong so you can take a pill or have an operation, have it fixed, and all will be well. Sympathise with their frustrations and pain. My husband is amazing at this because he's uniquely living the same emotions with me but he's able to be level-headed and almost has an outside view about the whole situation.

"Let's take a break." He said. Enjoy Christmas, take a year out to live and try again a bit later on. He was right. He knows me well enough to know when to step in. To walk away from all of it was absolutely the best thing to do. In that time, I came across a bible story/verses which made perfect sense to me. You don't have to be a believer to be able to identify with what this particular segment is trying to say.

Hannah in the bible was infertile. The story goes, she was at a banquet, everyone's happy living it up partying and she's sat there depressed because she was childless. Not only that, her husband's 'second' wife (that's what they did in those days!) was extremely fertile and mocked her infertility. How evil is that!? (Yes, I know what you're saying – 'but you have a child!' Yes, miraculously I do, and I'm beyond grateful for that every moment of everyday but that doesn't take away the pain you experience with secondary infertility and loss.) Hannah then, in a moment of exasperation, gets up from her seat and goes to the holy temple to scream/shout at God.

1 Samuel 1 V9-19 (Paraphrased)

'After drinking and eating Hannah rose. She was deeply distressed and prayed and wept bitterly. "I have been pouring out my soul, I have been speaking out my great anxiety and distress." Then she went her way, and her face was no longer downcast.'

This was a turning point for me, and it could be for...

1) She ROSE – don't allow yourself to wallow in your feelings endlessly, be proactive to deal with them.

2) She POURED OUT her soul – Whether this be to God himself, your family, a trusted friend and/or a professional counsellor. Let out your feelings and emotions 100% honestly. Please do it. Make sure it's with people who genuinely care and have your best interests at heart to guide you properly.

3) She WENT her way... NO LONGER DOWNCAST – Whether it's the relief that comes from sharing or getting help, also make a point in that moment to choose life. Choose to live and not be sad any longer. Of course, your loss will always be part of you but when you're ready, choose to make peace that it was totally out of your control. Remember those who love you and remember your self-worth – to love

yourself. Choose this day to step forward and begin again.

Another metaphor for this is stepping out of a boat. You can see the place you want to be but you're sacred to make that step. Yes, the boat in comfortable, you feel safe within yourself there and you're going to get your feet wet if you make that step forward. It may be cold, uncomfortable and painful at times. You may need to swim and really push through those tides at times to keep afloat but keep your eyes fixed on that sandy calm beach ahead. For then and only then, when you reach it, you can stop struggling. Your feet will be on solid ground once again and you can be at peace enjoying the warm sunshine on you face.

Chapter Ten – Going private, Going again

A year or so went by and we did, indeed live. We realised we didn't want our pain and longing to overshadow the childhood of our daughter. There was a real potential that, if we didn't address our desperation and anger, we could ruin her precious younger years and it would be too late to get them back. We planned days out and holidays, anything that could create amazing memories as a family because, after all, our daughter really was the gift we never thought we'd have, and we weren't going to waste a second with her. If you ever get to read this my gorgeous girl – you are loved more than you could ever know, and we feel the luckiest people in the world to call you ours. You are our everything – no matter what, always and forever.

Towards the end of 2021 our longing for a sibling for our daughter came creeping back again. She would come home from school asking when she was going to get a sister or brother like her friends. You know, the usual kid's questions that were very hard to answer simply! So, we decided to go the route of tracking my ovulation. If you've not done this before, it's where you pee on a stick (similar to pregnancy tests) and the darker the second line gets, it means your hormone surge, to release an egg, is going to happen within the next 24-48 hours. I understand, especially if you've been doing things this way for a while, it can lead to 'organised' love making or, some say, 'robotic' if the moods not there. But we found, when you both want the same thing, you can overcome this. Make it fun, don't make it all business, as a couple you can figure that one out. Sorry Dad if you're reading this!

You see, according to the science, once the egg is released it only has a very small window to be fertilised – less than twenty-four hours to be exact! So, you need to get it right…. Having some swimmers ready in waiting to go before the surge is also preferable. Remember sperm last up to five days in the womb so as soon as the second line begins to darken, go for it every other day (as every day can deplete you man's supply and doing the deed every day can get exhausting!) and then for sure once both lines are bold and the same in colour and appearance.

For us, even giving this a go for some time didn't lead to any pregnancies. The good thing about ovulation strips is it enables you to feel you have some control over a situation where you feel like you have none. Getting a positive line on an ovulation test is a welcome joy to the years of negative one liner pregnancy results and it feels you with a kind of hope. But it doesn't take away the agony of the 'two week wait' (the stage between ovulation and your expected menstruation date) or the pain when you don't get a positive pregnancy test and your 'Auntie Flo' arrives. You must stay hopeful and remind yourself that, if your periods are regular and you've had testing like myself, then you know you're a healthy human being and that's something to be celebrated. After a year of this though, that mentality wasn't enough for me and we considered our next move. The NHS, at that time, could do no more for us. As far as they were concerned, they had done all the checks for my miscarriages and they wouldn't give us any fertility support because we had our daughter. To be fair, this is completely the correct response – the funds SHOULD be reserved for those who are childless, they are the ones who deserve it most. But it's always worth having a chat with your GP to see what your options are with regards to fertility support, no matter your circumstances.

We chose to go to a fertility specialist privately. I still had too many questions. Why was I experiencing secondary infertility? Was my husband's sperm now of slow/bad quality? Was I running out of eggs? Were they bad quality? What about my general heath? How was my thyroid? My hormone levels? Was I making enough progesterone to support a pregnancy? Was I ovulating properly every month? Could they suggest something I was missing? I consider myself one of the lucky ones because we had savings we could use for this. We knew it was going to be costly - £2,000 near enough and we decided for peace and closure once and for all, it was worth it. Also, since covid restrictions were being lifted, we could finally do something together!

"I owe you an apology." I said to my long-time friend (the one who amazingly guided me through my grief.)

"Really? Why?" she asked.

"I used to look at you when you'd walk out of the room during a pregnancy announcement or when a new born was close by. I would say to my husband – 'what's her problem? She has her son! What's she got to be sad about?' I apologise because now I totally understand."

I don't want my daughter to be alone. I really want her to have a sibling. I have a brother and a sister, and my husband has a brother. We both come from substantially large families so having an only child felt almost unnatural compared to our childhood environments. We wanted to do all we could to figure out what was going on so that in the future we could tell our daughter we did every test, every treatment, within the frame of what felt was right for us, to give her that sibling we all wanted. We made an appointment to speak with a fertility specialist in Dorset. His clinic was one we had gone to in the past to have a 3D scan of our daughter, so we were familiar with its standards and felt comfortable to proceed with revealing our deepest desires and struggles with them. I would say, if you're going to go private for any fertility tests and treatments – do your research. Make sure they're 'legit'. Maybe ask other women for recommendations and know exactly what you want out of it, otherwise you may find your funds run away from you.

The doctor we saw was lovely. He was really approachable in his manner, someone we respected for his years in the profession, and he wasn't pushy with procedures or additional examinations/suggestions. We gave him our complete back story and I could see on his face he was as perplexed as we were.

"We need to get a full picture here." He said. And we agreed. I'd had the miscarriage tests, they were all clear, so it was down to my general health and that of my husbands that needed a deeper look into. I was booked in for an ultrasound to examine all my 'female' areas for anything untoward and to have several blood tests. These would indicate what my hormones and thyroid were doing at different points of my cycle and if they were at the level's they should be for that stage. It was a lot of going back and forth to the clinic, which is something to consider if it's not somewhere local to you, as I had to be present for these things to be done at the exact time of each phase. Then my husband got his swimmers checked out, this being the only test that was required of him! How unfair! Hang on a minute… are you getting a sense of déjà vu?! Because I certainly am! Oh, to be a man in a man's world!

We had a zoom consultation going over all the results in a matter of weeks.

"Everything looks great. Your womb and ovaries are healthy, no signs of any genealogical conditions. Your hormones are perfect, you're ovulating normally. Your progesterone levels are good. Also, from the scan, we can see you had a good number of eggs and your reserves are good too. All is as it should be. Your partners sperm has come back as adequate, so although it's not super fertile, it's still good quality and speed, nothing that would be cause for concern. At this point I would normally recommend an HSG procedure (checking the fallopian tubes for blockages) but because you've had that done in the past, and more importantly, been pregnant recently, I don't believe it's needed."

He paused.

"I can totally understand this is not what you wanted to hear. It's frustrating. We don't know why you keep losing babies and now you're experiencing difficulties getting pregnant again. But it's all a game of transport."

"Transport?" We asked.

"Yes. We can test everything to our knowledge as specialists and try and make these things happen but it's up to the sperm and the egg to make the journey. If everything is working as it should, the sperm should meet the egg and the fertilisation should happen, but it doesn't always work out that way. We can try IUI (where the sperm is inserted into the fallopian tube at ovulation time) to cut out the 'journey' but we don't do this here and the success rates are very low. You could have your DNA/chromosomes looked at by a specialist but again, we don't do this here and it is very expensive."

We were feeling more and more disheartened.

"At this point I would normally recommend IVF as the next step but in your case, I wouldn't recommend this."

"Really?" we said. For someone who runs a fertility clinic we were very aware he could be quick to jump on the IVF train because it's what brings in the big bucks for these places. But he was actually putting MY health first, which to me was a huge emotional moment and I felt overwhelmed by his care.

"You're healthy. You're ovulating normally. Your eggs are good, your hormones are where they should be. If I were to do chemical IVF you would be on ovulation stimulants and have to use other forms of hormonal injections throughout. You would be over stimulating your ovaries, and this could potentially make you very sick (ovarian hyperstimulation syndrome) and cause the opposite of what we're trying to achieve. This would be unsafe, and I wouldn't recommend you go for this."

I had kind of come across this whilst watching The Kardashians (Sorry – but I love watching that show!) Kourtney and her now husband, with all the money in the world, were trying to have a baby and had started IVF. They had tried all sorts of natural remedies and regimes to no avail, so went the chemical route. All the drugs she was getting didn't help at all to get her body where it needed to be for egg retrieval and was actually causing her to go into early menopause. As I've said before, with them having endless funds to draw on, they still couldn't get a healthy egg for some months and when they did, it wouldn't develop enough for implantation. It was really refreshing to watch because normal people could only dream of having the connections they do and they luxuries they can obtain. Yet here was someone who had three kids, millions of pounds in the bank and still she couldn't make life happen for her. I really felt for her. She was very brave to share her journey with entire world on TV!

It doesn't matter what the circumstances are, when you want a child so badly and it doesn't happen – It's the worst feeling in the world. It's heart-breaking, especially when there's so many women out there who get pregnant 'accidently' or don't want them. (I'm not going to get into that debate as this is a personal expression and I understand everyone's circumstances are individual and their own journey is something I have no right to judge on). It's just a gut-wrenching feeling, mixed with anger and pain that only someone who goes through infertility understands.

Back to the specialist...

"Look, you're both healthy, both still young. Keep taking supplements, have regular rolls in the hay and it should happen for you. You could look at having another HSG (fallopian tube check) later on just to double check there's been no damages or blockages since your last miscarriage and then IUI should you wish to give something a go at least."

We looked at one another.

"I think after all the losses we've had and going through another battery of tests we're going to take another break."

"I think that's very wise." He replied. "In the meantime, I'm going to prescribe you progesterone pessaries. I know that your hormones are normal but WHEN you fall pregnant it could help things along for you. It won't harm the baby and get in touch with us for an early pregnancy scan."

I was blown away. I hadn't said anything about what the midwife at the women's hospital said to me after I lost our baby in the summer before. But here he was, saying what I thought the gynaecologist in the hospital should have said to me when giving me my miscarriage results. I know that the progesterone drugs were no sure thing, but he was giving me the support I desperately needed. That if I did fall pregnant again, I could do something proactive to potentially to save my babies life. The other thing that struck me when he spoke was his use of tensing… 'WHEN'. There was no 'if' or 'maybe', he believed I would and could have another baby. That gave me something much more than any drug or examination could, just like that one midwife the year before had done also, it gave me – HOPE.

Hope for the future, whatever that may be.

Chapter Eleven – To the future – to the unknown

It's now early 2023 and I'm coming to the end of writing this book. It's taken me a long time and taken a lot out of me to relive a lot of memories. It's certainly not the end of my story.

Just in the news recently, they've made it mandatory for all healthcare professionals to be trained in women's health. Specifically, endometriosis, HRT treatments and menopause. But most amazingly, all women will now get a certificate of life for any child lost before birth. What an incredible acknowledgement of life, love and loss! I appreciate some women will not want this. I have met individuals who have experienced different stages of miscarriage and sometimes they can take it or leave it. Perhaps this is a coping mechanism, or they don't want to acknowledge their loss? Or a way to hide their grief? Perhaps they simply see a loss as very matter of fact. But as my book is evident of this, all women react differently to losing a child at any stage. We need to respect that and support them in the way they specially want to be.

Also, thanks to the charity Tommy's, the government is looking to reduce the threshold for number of miscarriages in order to access testing earlier. After all, three in a row is far too many losses to endure, to meet the criteria for simple investigations and is, after all, only experienced by 1% of couples!

We are still not pregnant, we're always trying in a relaxed manner and for us, that's ok. We had a quote through for an HSG test (fallopian tube check) and briefly had a look at natural IVF (Egg collection and implantation without the use of any drugs). But the cost of living is raging, and we need to protect our finances and our savings. HSG costs around £500 and natural IVF is still relatively the same cost as normal (chemical) IVF, not including the petrol costs of coming and going to the clinic each time. It's a lot to consider for anyone.

Recently we came to the realisation that even if we went against the specialists' recommendations and did IVF, (or any other form of fertility treatments) it was still up in the air if I would even be able to carry a fertilised egg to term. I would now be considered as high risk and nothing was going to change that. There was still no explanation for why I kept having miscarriages. At nearly £3,000 a cycle, even one try was enough for our finances and even then, we weren't guaranteed it would work out anyway. Our thoughts went back to the conversation we had before we approached the clinic – we don't want to waste our daughter's childhood (and potentially her future) spending it on focusing all our energy and money on having another child. What about her? She would be missing out on us both physically and emotionally if we gave ourselves over to cycles of IVF. Were we comfortable with this? The answer for us was no.

I still ponder on our journey. How is it that so many women can get pregnant...? When you think of all the things that have to line up perfectly at one time for life to happen, it's a miracle every single one of us are here. I thought about the obsessive ways in which I looked after myself taking supplements, changing my diet, sometimes obsessively when others, who aren't even trying to conceive, live really unhealthy lifestyles, drink excessive alcohol, sometimes taking drugs and still they get pregnant and carry a child to full term. It still baffles me. It just goes to show that we can try and make things happen on our own terms but sometimes life is uncontrollable. Things do and don't happen for a reason and although we can't make sense of it, we should choose to be grateful for the things we do have and make peace with the things we don't. We may re visit adoption in the future but with the age my daughter is right now, we just don't feel the time is right and she is not in a place to fully understand what that involves. Should we not have miraculously been able to have our daughter then 100% we would have adopted by now. We could not have lived or lives without a child. We knew that from day one.

Will we ever get the rainbow baby (a child born after a loss/multiple losses) we so desperately want? It seems everyone around us that had experienced a miscarriage has, so why not us?

But here we are now in this moment and we have been given an indescribable gift, a daughter, (even though I still can't grasp how she's here!) that many others don't get to have. She is amazing and I don't want to miss a single second of her life. So, in conclusion, we are going to stop 'trying', not have any more tests, not try and make life happen because there's too many uncertainties around loss and has the potential for it to completely take over our lives in a negative way. Perhaps in a few years' time we will do a few simple blood tests again and think about getting my tubes checked if I've still not managed to fall pregnant again, but we shall see what the future brings. We have come full circle and accept that, because we are completely healthy, maybe randomly one day we will have another but if we don't then that's ok. I will stop checking every month for that positive line and live my life enjoying the incredible family I have been given. I will count my blessings daily. Yes, I know there will be times when things come to bite me in the bum with memories or a reminder of pains I have gone through but that's ok too. My losses will never leave me, and I don't want them to because they are mine. I still won't wear tight fitting clothes for fear of my usual womanly bloating leading to people asking if I'm expecting. It's a small way to protect myself from opening up a can of worms of emotions that don't necessarily need to be awoken. I know my PND massively changed me, my painful experiences changed me and so did me questioning my own existence at times. But I know now that if I wake up and I'm having bad day, its ok to say no to things, it's ok to be a little bit selfish if it means waking up the next day feeling better. I recognise now when things are getting too much for me and when to take a step back or know beforehand what I can and can't manage sometimes. I'm thankful that I didn't act in my desperations but took wise counsel and took the time I needed to get better. Because I'm proof that even through all the hard times, some of which were truly terrible and to some perhaps a lost cause, you can come out the other side and be yourself again. It may not be the same you as before everything you'd gone through, but you will be wiser, stronger and more empathetic. This is why I wrote my story down. For others out there going through the endless infertility black hole, post-natal depression upheaval or multiple losses. Perhaps my experiences can help guide you in a positive way through what are truly challenging subject matters. If I can hit rock bottom and be ok again, so can you. If I can face heart-breaking grief and be ok, so can you and if you're facing decisions on fertility and don't know what to do next, my hope is that my journey can help make you feel ok too – or my wish for you – to feel/be empowered.

There WILL be good times ahead, that is a promise and although your wishes may not come true how you thought they would, it doesn't mean they can't in other ways. They could be even better than you could ever have imagined. Just chose today to find your peace, to remain steadfast and to, most importantly, live.

Charities and Helplines

- Your GP
- NHS 111
- Your Local Women's Hospital
- Your Local A&E

- Fertility Network UK

www.fertilitynetworkuk.org

Info: 01424 732361

Support Info: 0121 322 5024

- MIND (Mental Health Charity)

www.mind.org.uk

Info: 0300 123 33983

- SHOUT (Emergency Mental Health Support)

Text: SHOUT to 85258 (Free 24hrs/ 7 days a week)

- SAMARITANS

Call: 116 123 (365 days/24hrs Free)

Samaritans SELF HELP APP

FREEPOST to Samaritans letters

- Adoption UK (BARNARDOS)

www.barnardos.org.uk

also;

Your Local County Council Website (search Adoption)

- Miscarriage Association

Info@miscarriageassosiaton.org.uk

Helpline: 01924 200799 (Mon- Fri 9am-4pm)

- SANDS   (Saving babies. Supporting bereaved families)

Helpline: 0808 164 3332

helpline@sands.org.uk

- TOMMYS   (Charity. Together, for any baby)

Baby loss support online information

Online Support Groups

midwife@tommys.org or 0800 014 78000

 Birthing Pains Facebook Page

For relevant subject updates and support

Printed in Great Britain
by Amazon